The ART of FALLING

Lessons from a lifetime of trips, slips, and faceplants.

Donna Oberg

Tellwell Talent
www.tellwell.ca

ISBN
978-0-2288-6591-9 (Hardcover)
978-0-2288-6590-2 (Paperback)
978-0-2288-6592-6 (eBook)

Falling

adjective
3.   1.
        moving from a higher to a lower level, typically rapidly
        and without control.
        "she was injured by a falling tree"

Contents

CHAPTER 1

Falling teaches you grit

My grunt and laughter were muffled as my face was planted in the pavement. Nice. Right in the middle of Palace Square in St. Petersburg, Russia. We had just visited the Hermitage Museum. My mom and sister hadn't yet realized I wasn't keeping pace behind them.

But someone did.

A Russian soldier witnessed my fall in all its messy glory. Did he know that was fall 8,000,001? Just as my entourage realized what had happened and joined in on the laughter, I suddenly felt a massive hand grab the scruff of my jacket, and without ceremony, someone firmly planted me back on my feet. Before I could even say thanks, he turned and went on his business.

"Я шмякнуласьлицом" is pronounced: "Ya shmyaknulas' litsom." (Russian for smacked face or faceplant.)

It was the 8,000,001st time I've fallen down in my life, and my goal is to hit 10,000,000. Easy peasy. You can buy a winning lottery ticket on those odds.

Falling down isn't as bad as you think. When you've hit the dirt as many times as I have, you soon realize your ego isn't that fragile after all. And you learn to carry Band-Aids and Polysporin.

I'm not bragging, but I've had some epic faceplants in many parts of the world. And because I've been falling my entire life, I have a different perspective on it than most people. I call it GRIT.

Why have I fallen my whole life? Because I was born with cerebral palsy (CP) and, well, falling is part of the territory. Not all the time, but a lot!

What is cerebral palsy you ask? Go ahead, please ask. I honestly love it when people ask. It shows genuine interest in learning.

Here are a few fast CP facts:
www.cdc.gov/ncbddd/cp/facts:

- It is a non-progressive neurological condition affecting movement and muscle co-ordination. *(It may be non-progressive, but I've learned that being hit by a car and getting older can make it kick you in the ass a little harder! More about that later!)*

- It is the most common type of motor disability in children. Even I was surprised that 1–4 children per 1000 are diagnosed with CP.

- 75% to 85% of those with CP have spastic CP, which means their muscles are stiff, and movements are awkward. (*These are my people.*)

- Severity ranges from mild—where you'd find it hard to tell without really looking or being told—to being non-verbal, accompanied by an intellectual disability and requiring personal assistance for daily living.

My mom noticed I wasn't moving my left side when I was about six months old. When she took me to the doctor and all the tests were done, the doctor declared I had CP and they weren't sure if I'd ever be able to walk or talk.

They didn't know my mother or me.

It took me awhile and many worn-out knees in my pants from crawling until I was seven years old, but I do walk and with a pronounced limp. My left arm has limited use but it's a great paperweight. After musing on my hand, a friend once declared, "It's not the craw, it's the claw!" We both howled!

My balance, as you'll learn, is unpredictable. Oh yeah, and I *can* talk after all! Sometimes too much and often unfiltered, much to the amusement and sometimes the annoyance of family, friends, colleagues, and leaders.

Want to know what my CP looks like?

This is Dolly and me going on one of our adventures.

Life is so good. I want you to see that.

Right now, there's probably something you're not doing because you're afraid of falling. Or perhaps you've already had a spectacular wipeout in your life, and it has ground you to a halt.

I have a phrase you may want to adopt. It comes from a place of grit.

What's the most important thing I've learned about falling?

Most people think falling is a weakness. But it isn't. Because if you've fallen, it means you were doing something and not standing still. I fall a lot. But because I've fallen millions of times, I'm no longer afraid of it. That's my definition of GRIT. And I want you to have more of it.

I recently asked my mom if I was a stubborn kid.

"You weren't stubborn," she said, "but you wanted to try to do everything the other kids did, and you usually found a way to do the activity in some form or another! You were determined, and I always let you try."

She could've protected me from the frustration of not being able to do everything or from getting hurt. She could've steered me to something easier, but I'm so grateful she didn't. I'm grateful she let me struggle and create my own way of doing things.

I wonder if she knew she was teaching me to become gritty?

Sitting on the sidelines has never been my thing. Cross-country and downhill skiing, waterskiing and, shockingly, floor hockey were some of my favourites as a kid. (Although I only got up waterskiing once with my late brother, Vern. One of my favourite memories with him.)

Of course, those gritty skills stuck with me as an adult. It helped me secure a long career in the corporate world, too, with one of the largest companies in the world. I remember when I was struggling to choose between two young candidates for a position on my team at work. A manager said to me, "I'll always lean towards the person who's had struggles early on in life than those who appear to have 'skated' through life." He wanted the candidate to have developed a grittiness early on because he knew it drove them to see challenges from multiple angles, work hard and not be crushed by failure. I agreed with him, and I chose the gritty candidate. (And they were the right choice.)

Luckily for me, I grew up seeing failure as a viable pathway to success. Whether we like it or not, grit doesn't happen in a life free of struggle. And grit gives you gifts if you're willing to see them.

Let's get something clear.

You are not born with grit, but you can develop it. Research indicates traits like grit and resilience play as big a role in future successes (academic and professional) as IQ does.

I was raised to have grit. My siblings and I won the jackpot with our parents. Both of them grew up on farms and were tasked very early in life with chores. They helped the family earn a living, and they didn't get to finish school. My dad enlisted young and served as a tank driver in WWII. When he returned and started a family with my mom, he worked two or three jobs to provide for their growing household. Mom tirelessly raised six rambunctious kids and, let's be honest, caring for a disabled child requires a whole different level of grit!

My parents on their wedding day.

Yep,
That's me,
the baby!

3 uncommon things I've learned from my parents

1. **You'll struggle, and you'll experience failure, but it will be OK because it makes you stronger and better equipped to face any challenge.**

I remember Dad telling one of his war stories. He was on one of his first assignments as a tank driver and he mistakenly drove the tank into a ditch. This was a delay the troop could not afford. His commanding officer called him over (I'm sure Dad left out the colourful language), but basically looked him in the eye and said, "Swede, this is never going to happen again!" Dad learned a hard lesson that day, but he did note that indeed, he never let it happen again!

True, this is a pretty extreme example of understanding the importance of failure's lessons, but the army was where Dad learned a ton of life lessons. So, when he had kids, he wasn't going to coddle his children. They would understand that to struggle and face failure is not what defines you, but you'll grow and learn to persevere when you face it head-on.

2. **Persistence is key to success!**

This is especially important for things you really want. It's as important as not letting failure stop you. Maintaining a practice of persistence gives you the courage to face things head-on.

Mom is the perfect example of persistence … her and that damn iWatch we bought her a few years ago. My siblings and I bought it for her in case she fell. She could access it easier to call for help, and it has an added benefit of a fall detector. (I've learned through experience your fall has to be pretty epic to trigger it to call emergency.)

Well, that didn't matter.

When she found out she could track her fitness on it, she hounded me to show her how it worked. She's now obsessed with closing all the activity rings every day! And last year when she hurt her knee that didn't stop her! Once she was able to manage her pain, she was at it again. She says I have to do it, so I stay healthy. She is nothing if not persistent, and she really does seem stronger than before she hurt her knee.

And just so I don't forget the lesson of persistence, I get these notifications on my watch every time *she* completes a workout or closes her rings.

The woman is in her 90s!

3. Pressing the restart button.

"Try it this way instead."

These were words both Mom and Dad would say to me when they saw me struggling or when I'd fall and was working hard to find a way to get back up. Whether it was mastering cutting my own food with a claw, putting shoes on my stubborn disabled feet, or rising up from a fall, they knew I had to learn to press the restart button and find different ways of getting things done.

They wanted me to understand that each time we fall down and get back up we have moved forward, even a little bit. We're not starting from scratch but from a lesson learned, and we gain new focus, if not direction. Every time we try again, we are closer to the solution, to success.

They taught me grit.

Do you feel stuck right now? Have you been shaken by failure or a fall? Not sure how to keep going or when to press reset or restart?

We've all been there.

Take a breath.

Ready?

Can you see how your failures were lessons that make you smarter? How facing things head-on and persevering through hardship and pain makes you stronger? How knowing when to restart and try something a different way is not just creative but a gift?

Grit means you lean into what's real

It would be a lie to say I haven't ever felt frustration, anger, or defeat. When we're faced with difficulty it's normal to feel a range of emotions like anxiety, anger, sadness, and depression.

And let's not forget about our favourite defense mechanism:

Don't ignore these crappy feelings but lean into them instead. Weirdly, it helps you to understand your emotions and discover meaning in the circumstances you find yourself in.

I get it. Life can be a real bugger, even with the small things. But we need grit for all of the different shapes of struggle we have in our lives. Sometimes, when I get ready for work and need to be quick about it, my foot tenses up, which makes it almost impossible for me to put on my left shoe. The harder I try, the worse it gets. Throwing shoes isn't the smartest thing to do because I'm a s%&t thrower and with my luck it'll boomerang and hit me between the eyes and make me even later for my meeting.

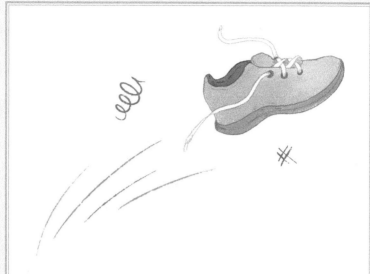

So, I've learned to take a few deep breaths to calm my heart rate and muscles. I tell myself to take my time, reposition myself in the chair and try again. Yes, I push reset. Usually, I'm successful and I fist-pump in the air like I've just won an Olympic medal! Who says we can't fist-pump the smaller victories in life too?

So, what's your word for grit?

As part of my research on the meaning of grit, I asked my social media friends to participate in a survey. They had to think of a word that describes grit to them, and the result is this cool word cloud.

Thanks to my friends who gave their ideas.

I know our eyes are drawn to the big words. Rightfully so. They are all great words and descriptions for what grit means, and the fact that most responses came within the first few minutes, makes it clear that many of my friends have pushed through difficult experiences and have recognized what helped them through.

Determination. Perseverance. Courage. Toughness.

But it made me smile when I saw spunk, moxie, and guts. These words may be simple and small, but they fit equally and are words I've heard often to describe me when I'm in the mode.

You too have grown from the difficult experiences in your life, just as I have. And if you're in one right now? You have what it takes to get through it.

I've always loved this quote by Abraham Lincoln. Abe's been dead a long time now, but his words have helped me scrape myself off the pavement thousands of times.

"It's not about how many times you fall, but how many times you get back up."

Don't we owe it to ourselves and our supporters to keep rising each time we fall? With each time we rise, we build the grit needed to get to the life we intend to create.

It certainly doesn't have to be pretty. Having grit doesn't mean you run as soon as you get back up. Often you need to stand still to get your bearings, scan your environment and check for alternate routes to your destination.

So, it's OK to ground yourself if you've fallen.
Take the time you need to gather yourself.
You can do it at your own speed.

Angela Duckworth, Professor of Psychology at the University of Pennsylvania and author of *Grit: The Power of Passion and Perseverance* developed a set of questions to measure a person's grit. My score was 4.5. Do you want to test yours?

www.angeladuckworth.com/grit-scale

Duckworth says, "When I get knocked down, I'll get back up. I may not be the smartest person in the room, but I'll strive to be the grittiest."

"Knocked down," "trip," "slide," and "drop, tuck and roll,"—it's like she ripped a page from my life story. I wasn't the smartest or the most creative in our family. I was definitely not the smartest person at school. But I've always been a go-getter! You know, the *get-er-done person*.

In my corporate life, I realized I didn't want to be the smartest person in the room because if I was, then I wasn't growing. I taught my team to be gritty. The final product/project may not have always been perfect nor pretty, but we were always better off because we tried, didn't give up easily and we reassessed and moved forward when we had to.

What are some of your best stories of not-so-perfect success?

When did you unexpectedly find your grit by saying, "What the hell," or even, "I don't give a rat's ass if I fall on my face, I'm doing this"? Or the time you realized you weren't the smartest person in the room and that excited you, it didn't make you feel inferior. How about the time you lost hope but then you found the courage to keep going? The time you saw your finished work of art, stepped back, smiled, and realized it was perfectly imperfect! It was good enough!

I know you've been gritty. You just need to think about it and remember. We can all learn how to be gritty. The amazing thing is we often forget the moments where we've *already* found it. You still have it. You've just forgotten.

So welcome to Club Grit!

Our motto?

"I don't give a rat's ass!"

Oh, and if my Russian is somehow reading this? Thank you Спасибо (spaSEEbah)

CHAPTER 2

Damn, that hurt

"Maybe you need to wear elbow and knee pads?" Fred asked after he scraped me off the sidewalk … again. Dolly ran circles around me, barking at him to pick me up, and she instinctively licked my wounds.

"You want me to wear elbow and knee pads to go on a walk? Not gonna happen buddy!" I snapped.

Was it my pride talking? Probably. But it was also the acceptance that living a life of meaning and adventure means bearing a bit of pain.

Life should start with the warning label: "Falling can hurt, but if you're willing to risk a few bumps and bruises, it is fun, exciting and an absolute adventure!"

The funny thing about my most painful moments is I remember *why* I was in pain and the lessons from it, but I no longer *feel* that pain. Pain is temporary, but it is a wise teacher.

Not all my pain or scars came from physical nose dives. Some pain involved my ego, my pride, and my thoughts. I'm sure you can relate.

There were times when I chose comfort over conquering and if I have any regrets in life, they are the moments when I lost that young kid's fearlessness. Sometimes, I chose to avoid the pain of the awkward and judgemental glances if I attempted to dance with my friends, or the physical and psychological terror of public speaking early on in my career.

As a young woman, I'd do everything I could to avoid business presentations. When I couldn't avoid it, I had a doctor prescribe me Ativan to reduce the symptoms of anxiety or full-on panic attacks.

Strangely, in normal life I felt fearless most of the time.

But put me in front of a group of people who were all looking at me? I became self-conscious of what people thought when they saw my disabled body in the front of the room.

My brave, "I don't give a rat's ass" mantra went right out the window!

I worried that being the centre of attention would trigger all sorts of physical reactions like tense muscles (not pretty with a spasmodic CP person), red face and quivering voice.

I didn't want anyone to think, *"why does she sound like she's crying when talking about profit and cashflow?* (Well, there were times when it would've been understandable.) The Ativan helped, but after I finished the presentation, I'd go back to my office and crash.

And then something wonderful happened.

I grew older and was less concerned about the corporate ladder, and I became reacquainted with that courageous kid who stared back at me in the mirror.

As I became comfortable with who I was, I realised *again* that I didn't give a rat's ass what people saw! But I wanted them to hear what I had to say.

I did some research and discovered most people are afraid of public speaking – in fact, of those people who are afraid of public speaking, 80% are worried about visible tremors, shaking or other signs of anxiety. I realized I wasn't alone with my quivering voice.

I threw out the Ativan and decided to just stand my ground and show them this Leaning Tower of Pisa knows what the hell she's talking about.

In life when struggle shows up – there are 3 choices.

1. **Quit**
2. **Live with the pain and move forward**
3. **Take your knocks but learn to be creative in how you handle them**

What would the literary world have missed if Emily Dickinson stopped writing when she struggled to get published? Imagine a world without Harry Potter! It could have happened if J.K. Rowling didn't keep going after the twelfth rejection from a major publisher. What if I had never seen the *Mona Lisa* because I didn't get back up after sliding across the floor of the Louvre as my mother and I rushed to see it before closing time?

Well, I certainly saw *Mona Lisa* from a different perspective.

As it turns out, the number of people crowding the area made the experience somewhat underwhelming. But I *was* in the Louvre standing in front of a da Vinci masterpiece. Brilliant!

What would you have missed if you'd ...

- *never asked or accepted a first date with your current partner?*

- *never said sorry to the person you hurt?*

- *never taken that side road on an adventure?*

- *never applied for your dream job?*

- *never forgiven the person who hurt you?*

- *never hiked to the top of the mountain you dreamed of?*

- *never asked that stranger for help?*

So, when you look at your "scars and bruises" can you see the moments you chose to take chances, to live your life? What if you saw them as symbols of courage and victory?

Fred had a point about the protective elbow and knee pads. Sure, life, with its falls and failures, can hurt. Maybe my stubbornness and love of living life to the fullest are my invisible protective padding?

You're no different.

Give yourself a pat on the back. You're tougher and braver than you think.

CHAPTER 3

Look for the helpers

I've always loved Fred Rogers aka Mr. Rogers. When he was a young boy, his mother told him if something frightening ever happened, he should: **"Look for the helpers."**

What a marvelous motto to pass onto a kid!

Luckily, my powerful mother taught me that I could ask for help if I needed it. (But she always wanted me to try it myself, FIRST.)

You're probably trying to get through too much by yourself, right now.

I think you need to look for your helpers.

At some of my lowest moments and after my most epic crash landings, I haven't had to look far for helpers. They are a myriad of wonderful people: friends, family, colleagues, and strangers.

I'm so grateful.

The expressions on their faces are clear in my mind:

1) The concerned smile.
2) The cautious laughter.
3) The shocked yet curious face.
4) The downright worried and mortified face. Yep, that's *my* Fred!
5) And one of my favourites, the Russian's. *Let's-get-on-with-getting-you-up-so-I-can-get-on-with-my-day* face.

I know you've seen one of these faces when you've fallen or told someone your bad news. And even if their reaction is hard to see, they're with you and you aren't as alone as you think. Sometimes, I see all these expressions in one crowd when they're standing over me. Someone has to break the tension, so I usually break out some smartass remark like,

"OK, who pushed me?"

Or

"Don't worry about me, I've perfected the art of falling."

But Fred brought something important to my attention after all my years of falling.

"You have no idea how traumatizing it is to see you fall and hurt yourself," he said. "It's not just about you!"

Huh. I honestly had never thought about it that way. Have you? He was right.

But you know who isn't traumatized when you fall? Dogs … dogs aren't traumatised. But they are there to immediately comfort you and alert others.

My favourite place to fall is at the dog park, although that might change if I ever land in the wrong spot. Why is it my favourite place to fall if I must? Because inevitably, five or six furballs come running over as if to shout out, "Hooman down!"

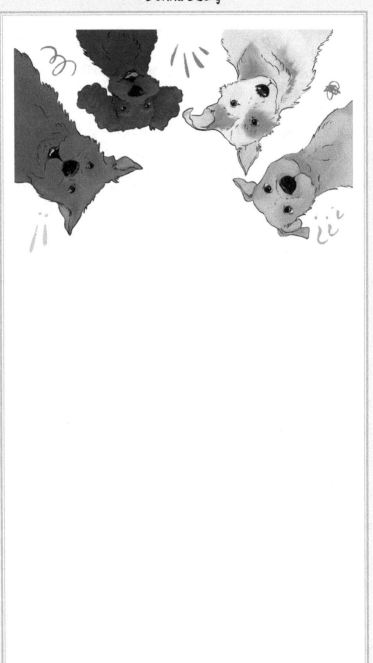

I can't describe the joy I feel looking up to see a bunch of furry faces looking at me with big panting smiles and wagging their tails! There is no worry on their part, no shame or embarrassment on mine. Just pure joy as I look at their smiling faces!

Is that why I didn't consider the effect of seeing me fall on those who witnessed it? Because when I saw the concern in their eyes, I focused on my shame and embarrassment? I'm not embarrassed when I fall alone, so why be ashamed when people see it and want to help? I think the dogs have been trying to tell me this all along.

Pride goeth before the faceplant.

All of us have experienced embarrassment or shame at some point. If you're human and breathing, you've felt it. Shame comes from our need to feel worthy, to belong, to feel accepted by others.

When I was younger, my friend Carla noticed I'd never look at the people who helped me up. A quickly whispered "Thank you" was all they received. (Well, I hope I said it.) But I wouldn't look at them. That was my shame showing up. Sure, I was embarrassed, but it also made me feel weak. It reminded me I was different … I was disabled.

How many of us have felt embarrassed after tripping on the sidewalk? Maybe we went sliding on ice and then glanced around hoping no one saw, jumped up quickly and got out of there as fast as possible. Phew, no one saw you right? Wrong. Remember the helpers are everywhere. They might not all come running to the rescue right away, but they are there waiting for the signal to help.

But asking for help is hard

As a kid and even into young adulthood, I would avoid asking for help like the plague. There was nothing worse than admitting I couldn't do something on my own. I paid for that in scrapes and bruises.

I'm not alone.

Sure, we all want to believe we can go it alone, but there comes a point when we must admit we need help. Believe it or not, there are people who are able to harness their pride, are aware they can't do everything and know when and how to ask for help. There are also people (like me) who had to learn the hard way first.

Not all helpers fly in wearing capes.

Helpers come in all shapes, sizes, ages and *even species*. Lol. And because I'm the expert at falling, I've learned loads about them.

1.   The Olympic Sprinters

You never know how fast people can move until you see them running over to pick your crumpled body off the floor.

I've even been helped by a sprinter 90-year-old grandma with a cane; 6-year-old kids; and dogs with tails wagging as they drooled on my face.

If you don't see them running, trust me, you'll hear them coming. They drop everything in their hands and instantly take off. Wow, do some people have heavy feet! With my ear to the floor, it can sound like a herd of elephants.

The sprinters are most likely to pick you up, dust you off, and then go on with their day.

And the gold medal goes to my Russian!

2. The Slow Mo Detectors

These helpers take a bit of time to register what's happening. They have a confused look on their faces followed by concern or terror. Maybe they thought you were going to catch yourself, maybe it looked like you were. When you didn't, they couldn't believe what they witnessed.

Once the fall registers in their mind, they check several times that you're OK and ask how they can help you. Once you're up, they ask several more times if you're OK, seemingly not believing you, if you say, "I'm OK." These people often walk away reluctantly and possibly more traumatised than you.

Make them feel better with humour. Like the time I fell beside a car. I slid under it and said, "I'm OK, I'm just checking the oil!" Ahhh, there it is … laughter. They will be OK now.

3. The Light Touch Helpers

These helpers may seem reluctant, and they are people you usually know. I've learned they realize I can get back up myself, but they always watch with a careful eye that I don't hurt myself in the process.

My brother Vern once emerged from an elevator in my apartment parkade to see me on my hands and knees, half in and half out of the adjacent elevator. My family was leaving after a Christmas holiday visit, and I'd tumbled trying to alert my mom of something she'd left behind.

Vern held a crossword puzzle and pen, and when he saw me on the floor he peered over his glasses and said, "What the hell are you doing down there?"

I was pissed and said, "I fell you idiot!"

Unfazed, he put his foot by the elevator door so it wouldn't crush me and watched as I pulled myself back up with the elevator bars. Wait a second. I don't think he even watched. He probably still worked on his puzzle. *9 letter word for fall: faceplant.*

Fred loves this story because sometimes when we're leaving that very elevator, he smiles and says, "What the hell are you doing down there?"

It's now a fond memory, and I can smile. (And I love you, Vern.)

4. The No-Touch Helpers

There are two kinds of no-touch helpers. They're either the folks who are so upset by what they've witnessed that they freeze and are afraid to ask you if you want help. Or they're the helpers who respect you need space. They know you need to absorb what just happened and assess what you need to do to recover.

I had a roommate, Ryan, who has the gift of appearing calm in any situation. Maybe you know someone like this. Skilled at being the silent helper, they sit quietly with you in your pain or sadness. They don't try to solve your problems but just be there in comfortable silence.

"That looks like it hurt. Need some help?" Ryan would say, calmly peering over his computer after seeing me drop unexpectedly.

I'd gasp because, of course, many times it did hurt, and I had my breath knocked out of me.

"Nope. I … I'm good … I just need to lay here for a minute."

Respecting my choice to handle it on my own, even when I was in visible pain, he'd turn back to his computer screen. But I always knew he had one eye on the screen and one eye watching to see if I got back up.

Sometimes the most powerful help comes quietly, almost unnoticed.

No matter which helper turns up, invite them in.

Feeling connected or wanting to feel connected is part of the human condition and is an important weapon to battle that shame I talked about.

When you allow someone to help, you declare you're worthy and that you deserve to receive, feel connected and be seen. When you allow someone to help, you're giving them a gift. Connections don't just happen when we receive help, they also happen for the person giving.

You wouldn't be reading this book if I hadn't asked for help.

Do you remember how much easier and how much more fun your project at work was to finish when you did it collaboratively? Do you remember the relief you felt when you told your friend you weren't OK and you needed to talk? Do you remember the smile on that person's face when you bought them a coffee at the local coffee shop? That feeling is the gift you give when you let people help you. No matter how small or how big the help is.

And if you've ever reached out your hand and scraped someone off the ground?

Maybe it was me. I'm sorry if I never looked at you.

I hope I said thank you.

Want to see the word for "thank you" in a few different languages?

Merci

Shukran

感谢您

ありがとうございました - Arigatou

Hvala

Děkuji

Tak

Salamat

Danke

ευχαριστώ

Köszönöm

Grazie

Takk

Dziękuję

Obrigado/Obrigada

Спасибо

Ďakujem

Gracias

Tack

ขอขอบคุณ

Teşekkür ederim

Cảm ơn bạn

CHAPTER 4

How to find strength in solitude

Funny how in a world of over 7.9 billion people, there are days when you feel completely alone. Hard to imagine that number? Check out this population counter and let it sink in:

https://www.worldometers.info

Even more mind-blowing is that there are 86,400 seconds in a day. Sure, some of that time you're keeping your roommate or partner up with your snoring, while you, of course, are sound asleep.

However, the odds are good that despite a crowded planet, you'll find yourself alone for some of those 86 thousand seconds a day. Seconds, days, weeks, months—there are times we need solitude and times when it's not our choice and it scares us.

I'm alone right now in complete silence, just me, my laptop, and my thoughts. Maybe you are by yourself too? Maybe you want to be alone but can't find the space or time. Maybe you're at the local coffee shop, sitting alone at a table on the patio drinking your favourite coffee, comforted by the sounds of laughter from the other tables.

I used to be scared of being on my own and would do my best to avoid it. When I moved to Calgary at 27 years old and bought my first condo, it was weeks before I had a decent night sleep. I'd never lived by myself before, and it was rare for me to be alone overnight.

Convinced someone would try to break into my 7th floor apartment (yep, that intruder would have to be determined), I wouldn't just trust the locks. I'd put an old metal cane in front of the door. In my brilliant mind, I figured if the door opened, the cane would drop and make a loud noise. Not quite as loud as when I tumbled to the ground with the cane, but loud enough that I'd wake up to call the police. (Big assumption here that I'd ever fall asleep.)

I might be the only one willing to admit I was an adult afraid of the boogieman, but I'm pretty sure I'm not the only one who set up these kinds of traps.

But it's not just boogiemen who drive us to avoid being alone, is it? There's more.

You worry you'll be bored on your own. Maybe we believe we need to be around people to feel strong. Maybe we're uncomfortable in silence. Could it be we're afraid to be alone with our own thoughts?

Check. Check. Check. Check. I have felt one or all of these things at different points in my life. Good news is I have no trouble sleeping now … well, most of the time. And having spent a lot of time alone, I now quite enjoy it.

Because part of the joy in the art of falling is falling in love with solitude. Meaningful solitude strengthens us in a million ways.

When you're bored, take time to create something or marvel in someone else's creation

Since I've retired, I've discovered a broad range of authors to enjoy, I've binged on multiple Netflix series, and I've done quite a bit of colouring. Yes, I said colouring. Fred even has one of my masterpieces on his fridge! And right now, I'm sitting here alone writing this book. I can definitely say I'm not bored.

There are so many ways creativity can be expressed. Perhaps you like to paint. Or maybe learn a new language so you know how to say "Thank you" when you get help. Are you a fabulous cook just itching to create a new masterpiece for your family? Many of my friends are bird watchers or gardeners, and they delight in being surrounded by nature and flowers they nurture to full bloom.

My sister Ingrid has a gift of taking scraps of things (driftwood, stained glass, tile, you name it) and transforming them into furniture and art. My sister Diana is equally creative.

Ingrid's scrap metal bouquet

Diana's driftwood face

I bet you have a creation of your own or enjoyed someone else's creation recently that saved you from the dreaded boredom. Sometimes while you're reading, walking, or slapping paint on a canvas – something amazing happens.

You discover you're strong enough to be alone with your flops and wins.

The connection you feel when you get a helping hand up is amazing.

> *Just as powerful is the pride and satisfaction you feel when you dig deep and succeed on your own.*

There is a time and place for both.

I don't always fall or fail in plain view of witnesses who can drop everything and come to the rescue. Sometimes I'm all alone in my apartment.

When I'm lying on the floor looking at the ceiling, strength doesn't always come instantly. Sometimes I lay there for a bit, tired of the process of getting back up.

You've probably felt that way too, but then your survival instinct kicked in. Just like mine does.

The instinct can start with the slightest flicker, pushing us forward. For me, sometimes the flicker is just my stubborn resolve that this will not be the way anyone finds my body. I laugh when I realize I'm in my underwear and think, *I'm not going feet first out the door in the B Team!* I drag my body to a chair or something else to pull myself up and dust myself off. First order of business is get some clothes on!

Many of your life's successes aren't always in front of people either.

Contrary to what you see in the media, not every success needs an audience.

Sometimes our strength comes at the most unlikely time or place. I bet you've surprised yourself at how strong you can be. When you finished the marathon in record time. When you faced your fear of heights and peered over the Grand Canyon. When you faced an illness head-on and won!

And let's not forget when you manage to open the pickle jar. All. By. Yourself.

Wow! You are stronger than you think!

Silence is a gift from solitude

Silence can be a golden ticket! Allllllllllllllllll aboard the quiet train. Sitting quietly and acknowledging the silence around you can recharge the battery of even the most fervent extrovert.

In a world that never shuts down and is almost never quiet, being amid constant chaos seems normal, if not expected. It depletes us mentally and physically, but we often ignore the signals and push forward fuelled by adrenaline and sometimes by coffee or the newest energy drink.

Worldwide, 166.63 million 60-kilogram bags of coffee were consumed in 2020/21 (Statista.com). In America, more than half of those coffee drinkers would rather miss a shower or gain 10 pounds than forfeit their morning coffee (*Huffington Post*).

That's just wrong!

Guess what? Your body isn't designed to keep going all the time. It needs you to stop. It begs you, and sometimes it forces you.

You know what I'm talking about. The times where you push yourself so hard at work, you go days without sleep, you don't remember the last time you drank water or ate. Did you even breathe?

Your body gives gentle reminders, but if you don't listen, you wind up wrapped in blankets sipping cold medicine or popping painkillers. Maybe you end up on crutches or, God forbid, you have to go to the hospital.

If you're tired right now, pay attention to that. Don't let silence be forced on you. Instead, embrace it regularly so that when it's time to call on your strength your tank will be full.

I hope you're curled up on your couch, with a glass of wine or beer or scotch, in your favourite loose pants, reading this book. Alone.

Congratulations on giving yourself permission to relax!

CHAPTER 5

A strange word you've probably never heard

Schadenfreude. It's a German word, and no, it's not breaded veal. That's schnitzel. Schadenfreude is when someone obtains enjoyment from the troubles of others. Say it with me …

/shaa·duhn·froy·duh/

It's when life trips you and someone else secretly enjoyed it. I don't know about you, but I've certainly been "schadenfreuded" a few times in my life. Maybe it's the memory you replay of the colleague who rejoiced in pointing out when, where and how you went wrong. They had a juicy case of schadenfreude.

But where do I receive schadenfreude the most in my life (and you too?) From the voice in my head. Martin Amis nailed it when musing, "The English feel schadenfreude even about themselves." I've nicknamed the voice in my head Cruella. Like the movie character, she's offensive and rude and drops by unannounced and definitely uninvited. What's your bully's name? If you haven't named them yet, go ahead and find one! It's a wonderful way to disarm them.

Make no mistake, you trip yourself up when you listen to this villain's crap or when they make you watch your failures repeatedly in your head. When I was younger, I didn't have the confidence or the weapons to get rid of Cruella. She was with me far too often and focused on making me feel unworthy and unwelcomed. As I got older, the uninvited arrivals became less frequent, but they've never completely stopped. I chalk it up to being human. I still hear her when I look at pictures of myself. Nowadays she focuses on self-image. I hear her when my eyes are (inevitably) closed in a picture or my hair looks like a rat's nest. I have an unconscious twinge when I see the effects of CP on my body.

All I see in this picture is my left hand.

You can't run away from the bully. Let me be clear, I literally cannot run away. But I've danced the Donna shuffle to distract them and focus on something fun! One of the gifts of growing older is your tolerance of the bully's voice wears thin. As you become more comfortable with who you are or who you are becoming, it fades and is easier to banish. Bullies run in the face of confidence. They can't handle the bright light.

You don't have to wait to be my age to get rid of the schadenfreude in your life. The cool thing about the art of falling is the realization that you have a choice today. You can face the bully today and show them the door.

How to catch a bully.

Keep an eye out for one of the bully's superpowers. Sometimes they morph and give you a nasty case of the imposter syndrome. We've all been there. You feel inadequate at a new job and don't feel smart enough or strong enough. It becomes a full-on syndrome when you convince yourself that one day the shoe will drop, your luck will run out and the dirty little secret that you're not as good as people think will be discovered. These feelings persist no matter how successful we become. Psst … you aren't alone; I've felt it. Many of my clients have felt it. The executive in the boardroom down the hall felt it. Around 70% of people experience imposter syndrome at some point. (Behavioral Science Institute)

These villains hide in the shadows, waiting to pounce when you least expect it. You can stop them in their nasty little tracks.

1. Don't deny your feelings. Instead, talk about them. Often just saying the words out loud can make them lose their power over you and set you free.

2. Don't try to be perfect. Literally no one is, and it wears you down if you try. Instead, remember it's OK to be wrong, it's OK to fail.

3. Don't put the recording on repeat when it comes to negative thoughts. Instead, start reframing.

Do these voices sound familiar?

I'm in over my head.

Everyone in this room is way smarter than me.

I got this job because I'm [fill in the blank].

What is your imposter saying? Write the words down. Really. Write them down.

Look at them and ask yourself if a friend or loved one said these words, would you let them continue to believe it or would you give them reasons to think differently?

Now that you can see those words in black and white, reframe them:

This job is tough, and I need to work hard and ask for help but I'm up for the challenge.

I'm so excited to be in a room of brilliant people! I'll learn loads of new stuff!

I got this job because of my fire and grit. Being disabled is just an added bonus!

When you take the time to reframe negative thoughts and start respecting yourself, I promise you the shoe won't drop or nail you in the head. It'll whiz right past you.

It's time to get reacquainted with the inner voice who counts. Perfectly messy you.

It's not as weird as you think. I don't know about you, but when I ask myself questions, I find myself answering out loud. That might be a tad weird. Weirder is when I tell my robot vacuum, *he's a good boy.*

It may help you to know that talking to yourself is common. Some people talk to themselves every few days, some do it every day (Sharecare.com). On average 60,000 thoughts pass through our minds daily, so it isn't surprising that some of those thoughts come from your inner voice.

See, you're not alone mumbling to yourself! According to a study done in UK schools, "Talking to yourself indicates a higher level of intelligence" (sites.psu.edu). Congratulations!

When you reflect on who you've become, do you see you're perfectly imperfect? What are your dreams, hopes and fears? What are your strengths and weaknesses?

When you hear your inner voice, listen carefully. If it's not being kind, then invite compassion in until there's no more room for her or him.

Even better, you just may find yourself in a wonderful place called forgiveness.

And it's closer than you think.

CHAPTER 6

the Forgiveness Café: A hidden gem that's worth the effort

My mom, sister and I were traveling to Florence, Italy, and my friend Adam told me I had to go try out the restaurant La Giostra. It averages about 4.5 stars, but the fact he called it a hidden gem? We made it a mission.

A beautiful, simple place waiting to be found.

We walked from our hotel down several dark streets wondering if we'd ever find this "hidden gem." After inquiring with a few locals and almost giving up, there it was. We had arrived.

The doors were wide open with tiny white lights flowing down all over the 17th century walls as if to guide us in.

When the friendly staff walked us through the doors, we realized this wasn't going to be an ordinary experience. After a full day of hectic touring and aching feet, the kind faces and peaceful atmosphere were just what we needed.

Not to mention the food was *delizioso*! The cheese and pear ravioli was simply amazing, but what we all fondly remember is the complimentary appetizer platter packed full of crostini and different toppings, exotically stuffed olives and a variety of carpaccio. OMG, so delicious!

Do you have a favourite hidden gem where the food is simple and amazing? Do you have a favourite menu item?

I have just the place for you.

The Forgiveness CAFÉ

Where everything is free

BREAKFAST
Benevolent Eggs Benny
Inner Peace Pancakes
Bacon Empathy and Eggs on Texas Toast

LUNCH
Rocket Relief Salad
Bully Bisque
Kindness and Cheddar Quiche

DINNER
Meat and Release Burger
Letting Go Liver and Onions
Savory Sigh Salmon

DESSERT
Gluten and Schadenfreude Free Strudel
Compassion Crème Brûlée
Freedom Root Beer Float

Vegan / Vegetarian options available

Careful. If you're not paying attention, you can miss the signs for the Forgiveness Café. Maybe you've looked for it before but gave up because it was too difficult to find.

This time you're determined. A few friends have highly recommended The Forgiveness Café, and the reviews gave 4.8 stars.

Who knew GPS can find where forgiveness is? Did you purposefully put The Forgiveness Café into your GPS, or did you just find yourself driving there? One thing is for sure, the journey to it is often rough and windy, so best to have four-wheel drive to get over the bumpy terrain. Buckle up!

The Forgiveness Café might not look like much from the outside, and it's simply decorated on the inside, but wait till you dig into the menu. There's a whole lot of goodness, and the staff make you feel right at home. It's as if you've always known each other.

This is not an ordinary experience.

Hope you are hungry! Let me share the daily specials!

Let's start with one of our healthiest options.

Savoury Sigh Salmon

Trust me. The first bite of this and you'll sigh with satisfaction.

Sighs are also a sign of relief, and we've all been there.

The moment you found out you passed your toughest class. C+ or A+ you passed! Go ahead, you can sigh.

You got the job you wanted. Time to sigh.

You were told you're in full recovery from your illness. Gigantic sigh.

You take your first step after being hit by a car. Surprised sigh. (Yes, this one is from me!)

The time you realized you found forgiveness. Not only did you feel relief, but the taste of freedom was exquisite. Go ahead, big sigh.

You've treated your mind and your body by letting go, without having to choose our liver and onions. (One of my favourites.)

Savory Sigh Salmon is a tasty healthy option with all sorts of benefits.

Next up is the Meat and Release Burger

It takes courage and strength to break free from the shackles of the past. This burger is just the trick with tons of protein. Go ahead—order it with a double patty! They love to please at The Forgiveness Café. And remember: everything is free and delivered to your table by me, myself, and I.

Don't mistake forgiveness for weakness. Forgiving is difficult, especially when you've been hurt by someone close to you. When you decide to forgive, you tap into your meaty inner strength. It's easy to stay angry, but it takes courage to face our emotions and transform them to compassion.

Go ahead, grab that double burger with both hands and take a huge bite. Don't worry about the mess.

Enjoy our all-day breakfast and dip your fork into the Kindness and Cheddar Quiche (you can follow it up with Compassion Crème Brule)

Today all items are also calorie free, so please indulge.

You never know what's going on in someone's life. Maybe they're going through a loss or an illness. Maybe, they were recently sideswiped by their own schadenfreude.

When we allow ourselves to believe most people are good and they have good intentions, we acknowledge that no one is perfect. We can look underneath the surface of their actions and see their pain. Perhaps we even feel compassion for them.

I get it, you might not be ready to invite them for lunch to share a gigantic piece of Kindness Quiche. It may take time and some boundary setting on your part. But one day, after enjoying your quiche, perhaps they can join you for dessert. Order my favourite, Compassion Crème Brule, and ask for two spoons.

Bully Bisque

I'm not typically a soup or bisque connoisseur, but this bowl of goodness surprised me and filled me up more than the burger.

I've had a recurring dream where one of the bullies from my youth tearfully asks me for forgiveness.

"I've forgiven you a long time ago," I promptly say. "I had to, so I could become who I was meant to be."

I say the person who needs to forgive them isn't me, but them.

Once, after waking up from this dream I realized I was crying. I realized I needed to forgive myself too. What? I know. We're all human, and I had to admit my hands weren't squeaky clean. I've hurt others out of my own pain, usually those closest to me. Because, of course, I know their triggers.

You might be one of them. I'm sorry if you are.

The person I really needed to ask forgiveness from was myself. Specifically, the younger me. I wasn't kind to her; I was ashamed of her and disappointed she was so different. I even wished she would disappear.

Thank goodness for her grit and warped, often dark, sense of humour. She used it to overpower the villain in her head. To overpower me.

I look at that younger girl and smile with pride and compassion. She sits across from me in The Forgiveness Café booth and smiles back. She's already forgiven me. She's finished her Bully Bisque and knows the Root Beer Float is on its way!

Your meal at The Forgiveness Café?

It's been paid in full.

CHAPTER 7

Falling gives you the gift of fresh perspective

Falling changes your perspective, both literally and figuratively.

I've seen many museums in many different cities while looking up from the ground. I swear some of the paintings of people looked down at me and wondered what the hell I was doing.

I've seen the faces and up the nostrils of people from many different cultures and backgrounds. Noses are like snowflakes, no two are the same. No two situations are the same either. Changing or shifting your perspective on a situation can be difficult and even feel impossible.

Maybe you're struggling with something right now and could use a new way of looking at it.

Well, one of the best ways to gain fresh perspective is to step away from what you're currently in. So, let's get a little wonky.

How about taking a masterclass on perspective from three of my favourite artists and one fabulous professor?

4 Art history lessons to use in life

Lesson 1: Look at it from all angles

"Stand in the middle of the room, move from side to side, or sit on the bench perfectly placed in the exhibition room of a museum. Whatever you do, don't just stand up close to the painting."

"Look at it from all angles."

I remember this life-changing advice from my art history professor, and I still use it today. I've lost count of how many museums my mom, sister and I have visited, but it's been over twenty for me and many more for my sister. (Sometimes Mom and I opted to wait for her and grab a beer at an outdoor café. A nice local beer can be another form of art to be appreciated. Salud!) When we do go with my sister, trust me, moving around the room to get different perspectives is a lot easier and less painful than doing a faceplant. Stepping back or sideways isn't just about seeing the painting or situation from the standard viewpoint.

It's about opening your mind to possibility, hidden treasures, and even lessons...

Move away from the chaos of the museum tour group who crowd and block your view. You'll see something you missed the first time.

I would have missed something interesting in this painting if it hadn't been for my professor's advice.

There's a da Vinci room at the Uffizi Gallery in Florence where many of his masterpieces are displayed.

Is this the path
you need to explore?

In the *Annunciation*, da Vinci inserted the nature element into his painting for the first time. Behind the famous scene, a tree-lined pathway slowly vanishes in the distance toward some mountains. Most people get caught up in the image of the Virgin Mary and the Archangel Gabriel without even seeing the pathway behind. Honestly, I missed the background the first time I saw it as well!

Before we left the da Vinci room, a group of students came in with a guide or a professor. He directed them to different parts of the room. I couldn't understand what he was saying.

My guess? He was telling them to,

> *"Look at each painting from all angles.*
> *You might be surprised at what you find."*

Lesson 2: Leonardo da Vinci, perspective, and the art of anatomy and sfumato

The second time I visited the Louvre in Paris and stood in front of the *Mona Lisa* my view was clear. This time I was also upright! As I moved around the room, her eyes followed me. Maybe she was worried I'd wipeout again and was keeping a close eye on me.

I've learned more about Leonardo over the years, and his life story is as fascinating as his paintings. Leonardo had a thirst for knowledge that spanned many areas of academics even though he wasn't formally educated. He questioned everything he saw and looked to the natural world for answers to the questions *Why does it look like that and How does it work?*

His curious and genius mind led him to excel in science, engineering, mathematics, anatomy, and proportion. His art excelled because of his knowledge in all these subjects. Strangely, he was a genius but still feared failure. Well, that proves it. He was human.

Luckily for us, Leonardo documented much of what he learned and attempted in a 6000-page personal handwritten journal. It has become as, if not more, valuable than his works of art. As with some of his paintings, Leonardo is thought to have tried to hide certain aspects of his work in the journal by writing in mirror script (writing from left to right. It is only readable if you hold a mirror up to the page). He even detailed a grocery list at one point, and it makes me think of my list (yogurt, eggs, bacon, bread) … oh sorry, back to Leonardo.

Leonardo noted that you could tell a lot about a person by their face. With his extensive work in dissection and anatomy, he declared it should be a goal of the artist to portray the inner thoughts and emotions of their subjects. He achieved this through facial proportion, expression through details of muscle and bone, and the technique referred to as sfumato. This technique entails the softening of lines between colours and shades to make sharp edges disappear like smoke.

And so, there *are* two sides to the *Mona Lisa* smile.

If you're too close to the painting and you look directly at her mouth, she doesn't appear to smile. But, if you step back and look at her eyes, the playful glance and the shading around her mouth create her famous smile. It appears she is waiting for you to slide across the marble floor and land on your butt in front of her.

Not gonna happen this time, lady!

Mona Lisa has two sides. So does pretty much everything in life.

In any situation, nothing is ever black and white because past experiences and emotions blur the lines.

Art shows us that to get perspective, you must look at the subject from all angles (even uncomfortable ones.) We need to seek out and listen to other people's ideas, thoughts, and opinions or suffer the price of only holding one view.

Listening with the intent to understand is priceless.

When you also take the time to understand the inner feelings and the thoughts of others (not just their words), stand in their shoes and empathise, it's easier to see there can be more than one truth, and it becomes simpler to understand how connected we really are to one another. This was evident in all the opinions and theories of the people studying da Vinci's work.

OK, maybe Mona was right to be a little wary of whether I would stay upright this time. I mean, first impressions are powerful!

The situation that you think you've looked at from all angles? Now it's time to go da-Vinci-and- Dissect-and-Sfumato-it.

Check between the lines, colour outside the lines, blur and soften the lines. Ask yourself why it looks the way it does. *Is there something I don't understand?* Pay attention to the messages hidden behind the layers and life becomes easier.

You're in da Vinci Mode. You're creating a new perspective.

Lesson 3: Vincent van Gogh. Create something to give you perspective

Oh, Vincent. I do love you so. Complicated, sensitive, kind, and shy with a soul filled with stars and sunflowers. He was so much more than the guy who cut off his ear. Before he started painting, he had tried three other careers as an art dealer, a teacher, and a preacher. After a brief period of success as an art dealer, Vincent eventually failed at all three jobs.

He had been interested in sketching and painting at a young age, but it wasn't until he was 27 years old that he decided to dedicate himself to a life as a painter. He had the full support of his younger brother Theo. Theo was his biggest fan, financial supporter, and his lifeline. If you're interested to see the depth of their connection, check out the 819 letters Vincent wrote, (most of them were to Theo):

www.vangoghletters.org/vg/letters

Vincent van Gogh was also determined to create depth in his paintings and drawings from the beginning. He struggled with perspective, as do most artists. As do we all. It's a part of being human.

At the Van Gogh Museum in Amsterdam, they are direct with their visitors and actively encourage you to view the paintings at different angles. (I know my Dutch friends are smiling at the thought of the Dutch being direct.)

They've procured a re-creation of the perspective frame that Vincent developed to help create his works of art.

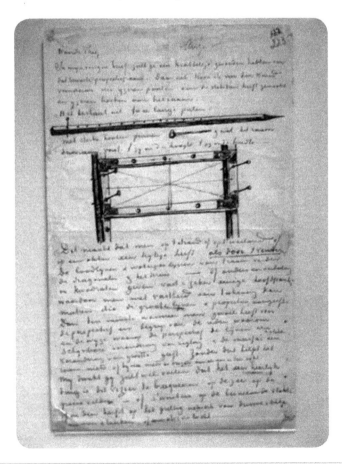

In one of the letters to Theo, he was excited about the potential of this frame and its strong wooden pegs and iron corners that would stand firmly in any terrain so that you felt you were looking through a window (Letter 254, Vangoghletters.org).

Some situations you find yourself in throw you off balance and knock you over. They change your perspective by the sheer force of what's happening. Finding an anchor like the perspective frame helps to refocus your gaze. It allows you to get your feet back on the ground ready to face the issue at hand. One anchor I use is to focus on my breath. It calms my mind and relaxes my body. My other anchor is to find the humour, even dark humour, in what's happening. Are these your anchors too?

Maybe you anchor yourself by holding the hand of your loved one. Maybe it's your faith. Maybe it's gratitude or hope.

Van Gogh didn't stop there in the lessons on perspective. Through his work over time you can see his shift in perspective on the world around him. I get it. There's nothing like time to soften our edges and help us see what's important through a different lens.

I realize now that the shifts were subtle at times in my life but no less life changing. Like when I realized I was no longer angry at the people who hurt me in the past. I'd forgiven them.

Sometimes the shifts were like jolts to the body. These shifts In perspective come in the form of a defining moment that challenges us to look at things a different way. They make us ask *Why?* and *What* next? They ultimately lead us to make a crucial decision that alters the course of our future.

For Vincent, each time he changed a career or moved locations, you can see the effects on him in his paintings. At the beginning, influenced by Rembrandt, his paintings centred around peasants and miners working in poverty and despair. He painted with gloomy, dark colours as seen in *The Potato Eaters*. I certainly didn't want to eat a potato after I saw this. (Now if they were fries, that would be a different story!)

When Vincent moved to Paris in 1886 and then southern France a short while later, he was challenged by the ideas of other artists such as Gauguin, and his colour palette became more vivid with reds, oranges, greens, and blues. The brighter colours in *Café Terrace at Night* and *Sunflowers* (which represented gratitude) are a noticeable shift in perspective from his early years.

Another shift in his paintings occurred while staying in an asylum after the famous breakdown that led him to cut off his ear. *The Starry Night*, with its dark hues, thick brush strokes and swirling skies, depicts (for some) agitation, chaos, and angst. Others may see hope in the stars. It's all in your perspective.

Vincent van Gogh's shifts in perspective revealed themselves in his paintings.

Yours and mine may be less public and less famous.
But time and experience has shifted our perspective too.

For me, the decision to retire was a process until I felt the jolt of a defining moment. I'd been feeling it was time to leave because there was something else I was meant to do. But it was terrifying to consider leaving a job that had given me so much and afforded me so many opportunities. People around me encouraged me to stay. They felt I had much more to do where I was. But then one senior leader who I regarded as a trusted mentor said to me, *"Why are they encouraging you to stay? Is it for their benefit or yours?"*

And lightning struck.

I believe each person's intention was good, but his question sent the jolt I needed to make the move and alter the course of my future.

I retired the very next day! Holy crap!

What defining moment in your life has shifted your perspective and altered the course of your future?

Was it when you lost your job and realized this was the opportunity to pursue your passion?

When you didn't win the competition you trained so hard for, or your project was cancelled at work, and you realized the world didn't come to an end?

Maybe you also decided to retire after a long debate with yourself and realized it was the best decision. Welcome to the club!

When sharing your diagnosis, you realised you weren't alone. You saw how many people were there to support you.

Look closely at those moments. See that? It's your perspective shifting.

Lesson 4: Frida Kahlo – Appearances can be deceiving

My first awareness of Frida Kahlo was that she was the Mexican painter with a unibrow. It made me much more aware of the need to get my eyebrows groomed on a regular basis. I didn't think much about her until 2019 when I went on a business trip to Mexico City. It was my second trip there, and my sister Lisa decided to tag along and explore Mexico while I was working.

As always, she talked me into a Sunday tour of a museum. We went to the Frida Kahlo Museum, which was where Frida lived almost all her life. Shhh ... don't tell my sister I'm grateful she talked me into this one; I'll never hear the end of it. Truth is, I'm so glad she dragged me to all the museums we've visited, but this one had a definite impact on me. One I won't forget.

Frida and I have things in common.

While I was diagnosed with CP affecting my left side as a 6-month-old baby, Frida contracted polio at age 6, and it affected her right leg and foot, resulting in a pronounced limp. She also developed grit at a young age, cheered on by her father. He encouraged her to swim, play soccer and wrestle. I bet if she lived in Canada she would have skied and played hockey. Her dad seems so much like my mother! Maybe they were distant cousins?

At 18, Frida was in a bus that was struck by a streetcar. This resulted in multiple fractures in her legs, collarbone, spine, and pelvis. Worse yet, her stomach was impaled by a steel pole! She was in the hospital for several weeks and bedridden for many more. Frida often painted her pain, and the effects of the bus accident are detailed in her work *The Broken Column*. She wanted you to see what was inside her body and spirit.

When I was 38 years old, a car backed into me while swinging into a parking spot. It broke my femur by my left knee and rolled on top of my right foot as I was tossed to the ground. I don't remember a lot immediately after the incident. I didn't go unconscious, but it's funny how I remember being on my back and looking at the sky and thinking the sun was shining bright that day. I was in a wheelchair for six months. Many of those days felt cloudy.

I had no idea when I walked through the door of Frida's house 3,925 km from my home that I would feel this powerful connection with her. Our disabilities wouldn't define either of us, but they did shape how we embraced life and our perspectives of the world. We were feisty kids who grew up to find our purpose and passion.

The room in the Frida Kahlo Museum that had the greatest impact for me was the room called "Appearances can be deceiving."

From carefully designed leg braces ...

… to plaster corsets painted with bright colours and poignant images that she wore with and underneath her beautifully decorated tunics and Tehuana skirts.

There was a full leg brace attached to those ugly shoes.

Frida hid her pain and disability under these works of art. Yes, she turned her disability aids into masterpieces. It wasn't so easy to hide my braces. I wore a full-length brace attached to an orthopaedic shoe when I was younger, and it could never be fully hidden under my clothes.

Mom tried her best to sew me pants to cover as much as possible, but I could never hide my twisted left hand.

If Frida wouldn't have painted such raw photos of her pain and the two sides of herself as in *The Two Fridas* she may have continued to *deceive* us all that she was always strong, passionate, and joyful. She was all those things, but not all of the time.

Just like you, just like me.

It takes courage to reveal our vulnerability. Through her art, Frida encourages us to understand that not all things may be as they appear. To look within ourselves to confront our pain and embrace our joy. She tells us to look deeper into the layers of life and our situation.

What are you hiding under your layers? Is it possible the situation you're in isn't exactly as it appears? Pull back the layers.

You might just find a new perspective that gives you clarity. I hope you find joy!

CHAPTER 8

Laugh on the way down

Something odd happens when I tell people about being hit by a car in San Diego. I can't share the story without laughing. Even thinking about it now and telling Fred I'm writing about it, we both couldn't help but chuckle.

I mean, really? I have cerebral palsy and then I get hit by a Toyota RAV4. Why couldn't it have been a Jag or a Maserati? It's important to always aim high, even in situations as crazy as this.

The whole situation happened quickly. I'd just arrived from the airport with my friend who I was visiting, and I got out of her car to wait for her to park in a tight parking spot. I stood where I'd gotten out to wait. I should've moved. I didn't realize she'd need to swing into her spot. Yes, it was my friend driving the RAV4.

Then SPLAT! I went down but it almost felt in slow motion. I heard a snap. I had no idea it was my knee. Honestly, I was preoccupied with the front wheel being on top of my right foot. Trust me, it's a shocking image.

What went through my head? *Crap, that can't be good*. And then I looked up and noticed what a beautiful sunny day it was! It's strange and beautiful how our minds will try to pull us from the dark and into the light to notice the brightness of a sunny day.

My poor friend! The situation was just as traumatic for her as it was for me by the look on her face. She was in shock, too, but it was amazing how both of us remained calm on the outside. We were protecting each other from our panic. We both went into problem-solving mode. The next step was quickly getting me up and to the hospital.

Later, when my friend and I were on our way back from the emergency department, I phoned my friend Peggy in Calgary and told her I'd been hit by a car. I burst out laughing. She went quiet for a moment.

"You're in shock!" she said.

"No really, I'm ok!" I insisted, still laughing.

Maybe it was nervous laughter. Was I trying to fool her and myself that I wasn't scared about what was happening? Probably. I wasn't OK, but I didn't know it until we contacted the hospital a day after because I was in excruciating pain, and I couldn't put any weight on my leg.

"Do not move her," the doctor said. "She has a broken femur, and you need to call an ambulance."

They'd tried calling me at my home number in Calgary and couldn't reach me because I was in San Diego and didn't give them my cell number when I was in the emergency room. Even *that* makes me laugh now. What went through my head was, *oh double crap, this is serious! In that moment I wasn't laughing.*

After I had surgery to repair my knee, the social services person assigned to my case walked into my room, looked at me lying in the hospital bed and said, "I phoned your doctor in Calgary today to tell her what happened. I told her you're in good spirits and you keep laughing. Your doctor said, 'Yep, that sounds like Donna!' She was used to me giggling relaying my faceplants, possible concussions and broken bones.

Oh black humour, I do love you so!

She also asked about my insurance because I had told her it only cost me about $25 for the four days I was supposed to be on vacation. She was hoping to get in on that deal! Hundreds of thousands of dollars in invoices later, and that $25 investment was well worth it!

To answer your inevitable question, yes, I'm still friends with the person who ran me over. There was no plot hatched over her morning toast, nor did I wake up that day thinking how great it would be to become a hood ornament. It simply was an unfortunate accident. Our direct contact has faded with the distance of cities, but we keep tabs on and wish the best for each other. Our story is a powerful one that connects us through the passage of time.

Hopefully you haven't been hit by a car. But is there a difficult time in your past that you now can laugh at? I hope so.

Mark Twain hit it on the nose when he said,

"Humor is tragedy plus time."

My dark humour is usually centred around my own circumstances such as a failed attempt to be a hood ornament on an SUV, doing a faceplant in a crowded museum or almost blowing myself up putting out a barbeque fire by blowing on it after a wind gust spread it to the gas hose. Right now, you're picturing me trying to blow out the fire and shaking your head. It's OK, I know it was stupid. We can laugh because I lived to tell the tale!

Laughing at hard times or awkward situations doesn't erase the experience, but it brings levity to stressful situations, lessens our anxiety and anger, and reduces our fears.

Confession. When a pigeon pooped on my sister in front of the Duomo in the Piazza del Duomo in Milan, I laughed so hard. In my defense, to lighten the mood I told her it was supposed to be good luck. Does that make me a schadenfreuder?

Although it took time for my sister to see the humour of her messy situation, my mom and I couldn't help but laugh for hours afterward.

Dark humour isn't for everyone.

Sometimes it's not easy to see the humour in situations, especially when you're smack dab in the middle of it. For me, choosing humour has helped find the light in very challenging times and dark days. Strangely, it helps to shine a light into the darkness, and it gives me hope.

Seeing the humour comes easily now. It's a choice I automatically reach for. Even as a kid I remember laughing a lot and trying to be funny. It felt good to laugh and make people laugh. It still does. I'm not disrespecting myself or anyone else by this choice. It's my declaration that I won't be crushed or defeated by tough moments, and my hope is you won't either.

We need to laugh more. It's something we all share across genders, cultures and even species.

Go ahead. Laugh like a monkey!

We are 30 times more likely to laugh when we're with another person, especially a person or people we know and like (ScienceFocus.com).

It indicates we share a common view of the circumstances around us. That may be true, but I've had some epic laughs on my own watching a funny movie, commercial or just remembering a funny experience.

You've laughed alone too. Doesn't it feel marvelous?

Humans aren't the only ones who laugh in social situations. Apes, chimpanzees, bonobos, and orangutans all laugh when tickled and make cheerful noises when playing to indicate they are not acting in an aggressive way. (Joseph Castro LiveScience.com)

And I swear my lovely dog, Dolly, smiles and laughs when she sees us cooking her dinners and when we say the word "park"! I looooove animals, and they've provided me with some of my most healing laughs.

Maybe don't laugh like an ape in public, but I dare you to laugh out loud next time you're in a crowd. Laughter is contagious, and you'll do the people around you a favour. They'll either join in or slowly back away because they think you're crazy. Either way, you win.

That's right, laughter is healthy for both the mind and body

Laughter triggers feel-good hormones called endorphins. A good laugh relaxes the mind and reduces the stress response to a difficult situation and even pain. Getting hit by an SUV that broke my femur hurt like nothing else I've ever experienced. But when I laughed? It helped.

I'm not suggesting you shouldn't exercise anymore, but hey if you're short on time, did you know a big belly laugh for 10 – 15 minutes a day can burn up to 40 calories? Annnnd, it leaves the muscles relaxed for up to 45 minutes after. (www.news.bbc.co.uk).

I don't know about you but I'm in!

My mom and I are PROS at this!

I'm pretty sure laughing is one of the reasons my mom is going strong in her 90s.

Laughter also increases blood flow to the brain and cardiovascular system, improving resistance to disease and sharpens creativity. (psychologytoday.com)

Laughter is your superweapon

When was the last time you laughed so hard you likely burned 40 calories? Or were inspired to create a masterpiece?

Count on kids to know the power of laughter.

On average a 4-year-old laughs 300 times a day, while the average 40-year-old laughs only 4 times a day. (psychologytoday.com).

I was skeptical about the 300 times, but I was just outside watching a neighbour play with her son, and he kept splashing himself with a bucket of water and belly laughed each time. They laughed at least 20 times in one minute. *I'm not so skeptical anymore!*

What happened to the other 296 laughs for the adults?

Laughter may not be your superpower, but it can be your superweapon both personally and professionally. When faced with challenging situations, laughter makes you more friendly, engaged, and optimistic, even if for a short while. It gives you enough time to get a new perspective on the situation. A perspective that propels you forward … potentially onto a new path.

I've always seen my odd sense of humour and ability to laugh at myself as my best weapon for coping with my disability. I can see the humour in trying to tie laces with one working hand and one claw. Getting through revolving doors without being propelled out and thrown on my butt is always funny. Faceplants? Hilarious!

Laughter is also my weapon of choice to disarm awkward, tense moments by helping others see the humour in life's challenges. I put people at ease around my disability by poking fun at it. When I can laugh at it, people around me don't find it so scary to talk about. They realize they can ask questions freely, and I get an opportunity to teach them about cerebral palsy.

My team at work laughed a lot, often because of some absurd observation one of us would blurt out. As I mumbled some comment, someone on the team would say, *"That's your outside voice, Donna"* … and then we'd burst out laughing. I loved hearing them laugh as they huddled together solving some reporting issue or, more often, the announcement of yet another reorganization. We started calling those days our own version of *The Hunger Games*. It made those days less scary. When they laughed, I knew they trusted each other. They trusted me because I laughed with them. We were a strong team. We had a superweapon and weathered a lot of storms together because of it.

So go ahead. Whether it's a small giggle or one of those laughs that makes your stomach hurt, laugh right now. You have 296 more chuckles to go.

CHAPTER 9

Gratitude and hope: the gateways to a better life

Some days I'm surprised at how grouchy, ungrateful, and judgmental I can be.

Like when my apartment elevator is out of service and I have an armful of recycling, or when someone pushes their economy seat back all the way on a plane. It's difficult enough for me to extract myself from the seat without trying to contort this disabled body to slink out and go to the washroom. (I know they're pretending to sleep when I tap their shoulder and politely ask to move their seat up.)

The Dalai Lama I'm not.

Yep, I can be cranky!

But the great thing is I know hope isn't lost, and gratitude is just one positive thought away. I'll always find them again because hope and gratitude feel much better than despair, anger and resentment. With practice, hope and gratitude can help you get through those moments when you just want to kick that passenger's seat.

Let's start with gratitude

"A grateful mind is a great mind which eventually attracts to itself great things."
– Plato

I'm a big Plato fan. As one of the most notable philosophers in history, he knows how to simplify profound ideas.

You might think saying the words *thank you* is an act of gratitude. But it's just the beginning. A good—no, a great—beginning toward gratitude.

By saying thank you, you express appreciation for an act of kindness or for receiving something that benefits you or brings you joy.

Do you remember why you said *"Thank you"* the last time? Did someone open a door for you when your arms were full? Was the grocery check-out person especially nice? Did your friend help you in a crisis?

Strangely, the words "Thank you" are the gateway to gratitude.

Gratitude is different. It takes time to develop, but when you achieve it, just as Plato says, you will attract great things. Sounds like it should be easy, right? Nope, not always. Sometimes you're just mad at the world. You were told your job was being cut, your health is suffering or maybe you just separated from your partner. How can you be grateful with all that going on? The answer is one step at a time, one act at a time, and one thought or word at a time.

I picture gratitude as another muscle in my body. I need to practice engaging my gratitude muscle for it to grow and get stronger.

When I'm in the gratitude groove, wonderful things happen.

Practice #1: Small steps can lead to big changes

Gratitude doesn't have to start with grand gestures.

The simple act of feeling the sun on your face, reading while the rain gently drops on your roof, listening to birds chirping (as long as they don't wake you at 5 a.m.), savouring every bite of your meals (especially that gigantic piece of chocolate cheesecake). All small actions of appreciation are based on noticing your contentment. Sometimes that's all it takes to start.

Once, when I signed up for disabled skiing lessons, I was walking amongst the chaos of students and their guardians, and I was frustrated by the frenzy of activities and being bumped into by walkers and wheelchairs.

Then I spotted him, and he transformed my day as I instantly moved from agitation to an attitude of gratitude.

He was a young blind boy, maybe ten years old, being guided around the room by his mother. He was silent and seemed focused on the cues his mother gave him to avoid collisions with tables, chairs, or people. Suddenly, he stepped into a spot in the room where the sun was shining brightly through the window. His serious face broke into a huge grin, he held his hand up and declared loudly, "Sunshine!" He felt the warmth of that spot of sunshine, and he was instantly joyful!

His happiness made me happy. And I was humbled too.

The big lesson he taught me that day is to notice the small things in life that bring me joy. To be grateful for things I normally take for granted. He brought me joy, and he reminded me of it too.

Was there a small ray of light in your day today? That's all you need to start. When you're mindful of the good in everyday life, gratitude becomes easier.

Practice #2: Gratitude is free. It's wonderful to give and amazing to receive

Studies show that just the simple act of writing a letter of gratitude and appreciation increases neural activity in the brain and sustains the feelings of gratitude for several months after (www.pubmed.ncbi.nlm.nih.gov/26746580/).

You don't even need to send the letter to reap the benefits. I know I said gratitude is free, but one stamp is pretty economical. So, when you're ready, send it. Better yet, hand deliver it.

Imagine what an amazing impact you'll have by letting someone know how much you value and appreciate them. You might just turn their day around or make it even brighter. Maybe you'll inspire them to write their own letter. Wouldn't it be great if someone wrote you a letter like that?

In his article, "10 Amazing Statistics to Celebrate National Gratitude Month," Cord Himmelstein noted some very interesting statistics including:

- "More than half of employees will feel better about themselves and even work harder if their boss expressed appreciation and gratitude for their efforts."

- "Gratitude from an employer is also an important factor in the decision of whether to stay longer with the company."

- "A daily gratitude journal can increase long-term well-being by 10%."

And did you know that November is National Gratitude Month? I had no clue. It's in my calendar now!

Practice #3: My personal favorite is to keep a gratitude journal

Each morning, while my mug of hot coffee sits faithfully beside me at my writing nook, and before I turn on my computer, I grab my journal and write a page full of things I'm grateful for. Some things are silly, like being grateful for pickles. Other are more surprising, like gratitude for my disability. With the balcony door open, whether the sun shines or I'm listening to the soft, comforting sound of rain, mornings are when I'm most inspired!

I am grateful for my
encouraging friends and family.

I am grateful for pickles.

I am grateful for my
mentors and coaches.

I am grateful for laughter.

I am grateful for my disability.

I am grateful for animals (especially dogs.)

I am grateful for grit.

I am grateful for
the lessons in failure.

I am grateful for forgiveness.

I am grateful for
my mother.

Believe it or not, a few years after being hit by the car, I even found gratitude in that.

Yep, it took many repetitions and some heavier weights, but the thing about exercising gratitude daily is that you open your mind to all the experiences, people and things that make your life better over time.

How do you feel gratitude for being hit by a car? More on that in a minute.

What are three things you are grateful for? When you're ready, start practicing every day. Even when it gets hard. Especially when it gets hard.

These practices aren't new, but the changes they bring to your life sure are.

Much of what I read on gratitude theorized that gratitude is the path toward hope. Maybe it's true in some situations.

But for **me**, after the car accident and thanks to my mother …

Hope came first

For weeks after the accident, as I sat in a wheelchair, I struggled to find things to be grateful for.

I certainly didn't have hope.

At one doctor's appointment they said they weren't sure if I'd be able to walk again. I didn't hear much after that. I fell into self-pity and despair, angry at the world. How many times would I be forced to re-learn to walk? I had to do it after each of my 4 major leg surgeries. I was much younger then. I wasn't sure this time I had it in me to do it again at the age of 38. I was tired of fighting.

You've been there before too. It's OK. We all have.

But I did have it in me, and one person knew it for sure. My 79-year-old mother who had watched me do it every time before. There was no way she'd let this time be different. Mom allowed me some space that day to feel what I needed to feel.

The next day, she grabbed the walker we'd been given, put it in front of my wheelchair and said, "Donna, get up."

"I can't!"

"Come on, get up."

"I CAN'T!"

She didn't skip a beat. With that look only a mother can give—you know the one, the face that says, *I brought you into this world, I can take you out!*

"YES, YOU CAN, GET UP!"

She instinctively sensed the fight in me was missing, and she knew she needed to reignite the flame fast to show me I was still the same gritty kid inside. Even if I only took one step. And then when I took four begrudging and painful steps? She offered to come live with me to help me get back on my feet. She certainly wasn't going to watch her independent daughter with a great career also lose her fighting spirit. She knew there was hope for me even when I didn't feel it. And let's face it, she wasn't leaving until I was back on my feet.

Now here comes the kicker.

My mom was 79 years old. In her third month with me, she turned 80. She was still incredibly strong mentally and physically. Imagine someone that age helping to lift me in and out of a wheelchair several times a day.

She's incredible. Absolutely incredible. And with her help, I was back on my feet six months later, so she packed her bags and headed home.

In spite of it all, I choose to be hopeful

My favourite quote is:

"When the world says give up, hope whispers: try it one more time!" – Anonymous

Hope doesn't mean everything is fine now, but it does make things less difficult to face because you believe things will be better in the future. Believing is key, because if you believe, hope pushes away fear and inspires you to work for and achieve the impossible.

> **"Hope and fear cannot occupy
> the same place. Invite one to stay."
> – Maya Angelou**

Hope's real name was Jane (I call her Mom), and Jane technically invited herself to stay. And for that I am forever grateful.

Every day after those first steps across my living room, Mom would put the walker in front of me and make me walk up and down the hallway of my apartment building. Of course, she'd do it after she finished watching her soap opera. No one was getting in between her and the next episode of *The Young and the Restless*.

This was our daily routine until I was back to walking with just a cane.

Five months after the accident, I saw an advertisement for the Mother's Day Run. I'd been walking quite well for a couple of months by then, and there was a 5 km walk-a-thon in the event. I thought, *What the hell? Why not?* The fact that it celebrated mothers also seemed quite appropriate given what Mom did for me over the six months she stayed with me. I recruited a few faithful friends to join me as a team, and I shamelessly hit up friends and co-workers to sponsor me. I mean, who's not going to sponsor the person hit by a car who worked hard to walk again? It was for a good cause, so I felt justified. In May 2007, six months after the accident, I crossed the finish line with my gang of faithful supporters. I was exhausted but extremely proud!

Mom has always been my whisper of hope helping to push away the fear and move me toward the impossible. Pushing me across the finish line. And she's passed the baton to me.

Who is your whisper of hope?

When I found hope, I found myself grateful for the accident.

Why? I knew I had fantastic friends, but the accident opened my eyes to the true connection I had with them and the strength of support they gave me every day with texts, calls and visits. And, of course, they walked side by side with me during the walk-a-thon and across the finish line.

Although I'm not sure if my friends were always coming to visit me or my mom. She became quite popular with the group. Her energy and sense of humour has always drawn people to her. Mom is popular amongst my friends, even the ones who've never met her. She's quite the star on my social media accounts too. When I post about her antics, she gets the most likes and comments.

The accident also reminded me how strong I am.

I am grateful

If you started this chapter excited about the topic, I hope you feel even more inspired.

Since I started writing in my gratitude journal, I've noticed significant changes. I feel lighter and calmer. I've repaired strained relationships. I see more opportunities instead of obstacles for the future. Things just seem better.

If you groaned, I hope your perspective has changed. That's what practice can do, and sometimes just reading about gratitude and hope can move you closer.

If you still aren't ready to let gratitude and hope in, I get it! Sometimes it really is hard. But when you're ready, come back to this chapter. The book is yours now. One day you'll be ready, and it will be here as reminder of how gratitude and hope are your gateways to a better life.

CHAPTER 10

Life's road trips: Destinations, detours, and discoveries

Roaaaad trriiiip!

Life really is like a series of road trips. I absolutely love them! Always have. My parents took a road trip each summer with me and my siblings, Bill, and Lisa, to Kelowna, BC. We'd camp for six weeks at the Happy Valley Campsite. The owners were family friends, and they always gave us prime real estate right off the beach.

Dad and Mom would set up the back seat of our blue Buick LeSabre like a bed, and Bill, Lisa and I would bring our favourite comics (*Archie*, *Spiderman*, *Wonder Woman*, etc.) and snacks (mmm Doritos) along for the ride.

We'd fight over who would lie on the ledge of the back window. Back then, the beauty of the passing scenery wasn't important to us. We certainly didn't pay attention to roadblocks or detours. Our parents worried about the detours, bumpy roads, potholes and where to fuel up. They understood the road was rarely smooth driving. Just like a life well lived.

We were also known to ask the dreaded, "Are we there yet?"

I remember Dad getting irritated at our noses in our comics and he'd say,

"Look out the window, dammit!"

All these years later, I still have to remind myself to not constantly think,

"Am I there yet?"

I know I'm not the only one. Are you paying attention to the experiences around you or are you obsessed on the next destination?

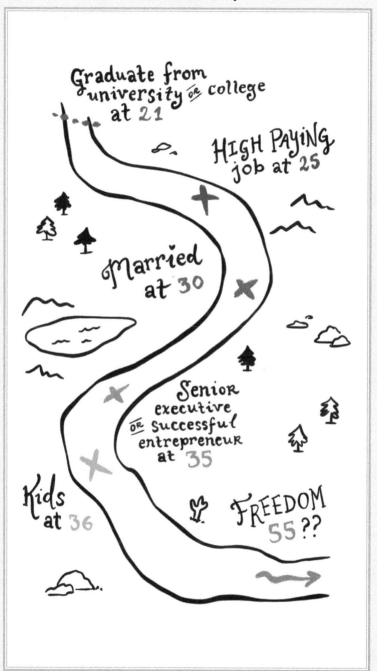

I've always been intrigued by the thought that goes into these plans. I've even felt envious of their certainty and resolve. When I was younger, it was never clear what opportunities were out there for people with my disability, so I spent my time figuring out my next steps one at a time instead of in milestones and giant leaps. I was busy falling, getting back up, dusting myself off and just moving forward.

Maybe this was why I find myself surprised when people never account for the possibility of obstacles or detours. Could it be possible they had never experienced one? The concept is foreign to me because my life has been scattered with both.

Perhaps that's why I've tended to be a fly-by-the-seat-of-my-pants person. Sure, I always had goals and ideas of how my life should go, but I've become a firm believer in expecting the unexpected. Not only expect it, but learn how to embrace it, because surprises can turn out to be some of our best discoveries along the way.

"Because the greatest part of a road trip isn't arriving at your destination. It's all the wild stuff that happens along the way."
- Emma Chase

So true!

A few summers ago, my friend Tony and I went on a road trip from Calgary to Montana. Our destination was Helena, known as the "Queen of the Rockies." As Canadians living in the Canadian Rockies, we had to check this out!

Little did we know the most memorable part of this spur-of-the-moment trip would happen en route to our destination.

Tony and I decided to stop at the nearest small town after crossing the US border with hopes for a good old-fashioned hearty meal. As we pulled up on Main Street, we spotted a diner with a flashing neon sign advertising it was air conditioned. Woo hoo! With growling stomachs, we walked into the diner eager to dig in.

The moment we walked through the door, the place went dead quiet, and all eyes were on us. Apparently, a gay man and a woman with a limp and claw were a sight to see. Both of us were surprised by the reaction; it was something straight out of a horror movie. No one smiled. No one greeted us. But we were hungry, so we sat down and ordered two coffees, burgers, and fries.

The coffee tasted like twenty-year-old cigarette butts, and the burgers … well neither of us cleaned our plate. We ate enough to fill the pangs in our stomach, paid the bill to the gawking waitress and high-tailed it back to the car. I can't run but I can move pretty fast when it's required! As we got in our seats and locked the doors, Tony took a deep breath, looked at me with a huge grin and said,

"That's the first time those folks have ever seen a gay guy and his disabled sidekick … let's get outta here, partner!"

We both howled as we made our way back to the highway!

In Helena, we found a pretty town nestled in beautiful countryside ("Queen of the Rockies"? Maybe not). What I remember most is the small-town diner, the expressions on the faces as we walked in and the amazing belly laugh we shared after our close encounter of the strange kind!

This is what Dad was trying to tell us when he bellowed at us to look out the window. He had learned that we're shaped more by the journey than the actual destination, and he wanted his kids to appreciate that.

My brother Bill has taken this to heart, and he continues the tradition of going on road trips with his wife and grown kids. I wonder if he's caught himself saying, "Look out the window, dammit!"

When you look back on your life so far, what experiences shaped you the most? Can you see it wasn't just the fun detours but the difficult ones that made you grow the most?

"Of all the paths you take in life, make sure a few of them are dirty."
- John Muir

I'm pretty sure my friend Andy lives by this rule.

I met Andy when I signed up for disabled downhill skiing lessons at Canada Olympic Park in Calgary. He was a volunteer, an instructor, and an avid skier with a speed demon attitude. Oh yeah, he also has cerebral palsy!

We hit it off immediately. His habit of laughing big belly laughs and his warped sense of humour matched nicely with mine. I knew we would become friends. He was like a male version of me. Oh my God, two of us! Look out!

Andy is no stranger to detours, bumpy and muddy roads. He purposefully seeks them out. He loves to go off-roading in this buggy!

Mud Loving Andy

The more challenging the road or stream to drive through, the more covered in mud he and his buggy get, the happier he is. I asked Andy about his love of off-roading and why he was so drawn to it.

"It was born from wanting to spend more time with my friends and the freedom of motion and adventure," he said.

He loves it, yes, but as with most of life's detours, it's not *all* fun and games.

"Donna, off-roading has taught me about preparedness, safety and how to solve a myriad of mechanical issues," he told me.

He credits these skills for giving him the confidence to safely get his family where they need to be no matter what obstacles are thrown at them.

And crap will happen. We all know that to be true. It's easy to stay positive when things are going smooth, going our way. But it's the messy parts in our lives and in us that help us to grow into the person we're meant to be.

Are you in the middle of a messy detour in your life? Do you feel you'll never scrape the mud off your face?

Andy and I are here to tell you that you've been preparing for this during every life road trip you've taken, and you have the strength to handle it.

Keep going. No matter how muddy you get.

**"Travel isn't always pretty.
It isn't always comfortable.
Sometimes it hurts, it even breaks
your heart. But that's okay. The journey
changes you; it should change you."
- Anthony Bourdain**

In life, we go through countless experiences, both good and bad. Dark and beautiful.

Our bodies change, and the passage of time shows in the mirror as we see our reflection. The graying hair, the wrinkles, and the scars. I agree, life does change you and it should. As I look at the road I've travelled so far, I can appreciate the pain and heartbreak. I smile and laugh out loud at the adventures. It was meant to happen this way, and it's made me this wonderful, messy person I am today.

The road trips you've taken have done the same. You have become the person you were meant to be. But you're not done yet.

And neither am I.

Rise
[rahyz]

verb (used without object), rose, ris·en.

to get up from a lying, sitting, or kneeling posture; assume an upright position: *She rose and walked over to greet me. With great effort he rose to his knees.*

Notes and References

The Annunciation – Leonardo da Vinci (1452 – 1519) - https://commons.wikimedia.org/wiki/File:Da_Vinci_The_Annunciation.jpg

Mona Lisa – Leonardo da Vinci (1452 – 1519)
[[File:Mona Lisa, by Leonardo da Vinci, from C2RMF retouched.jpg|Mona_Lisa,_by_Leonardo_da_Vinci,_from_C2RMF_retouched]]
https://commons.wikimedia.org/w/index.php?search=mona+lisa&title=Special:MediaSearch&go=Go

The Perspective Frame – Vincent van Gogh (1853 – 1890)
A sketch by Vincent van Gogh which represents his perspective frame
https://commons.wikimedia.org/wiki/File:Van-Gogh-Perspective-frame.jpg

The Potato Eaters – Vincent van Gogh (1853 – 1890)
Photo by Szilas at the Van Gogh, My Dream Exhibition in Budapest, 2013, Public Domain, https://commons.wikimedia.org/w/index.php?curid=31826077

Broken Column By Ambra75 - Own work, CC BY-SA 4.0, https://commons.wikimedia.org/w/index.php?curid=92964842
[[File:Mostra di Frida Kahlo al Mudec di Milano 3 maggio 2018 (21) (cropped).jpg|Mostra_di_Frida_Kahlo_al_Mudec_di_Milano_3_maggio_2018_(21)_(cropped)]]

All other photos and illustrations owned and copyrighted by Donna Oberg, 2021

Chapter 1
What is Cerebral Palsy?
https://www.cdc.gov/ncbddd/cp/facts.html

Chapter 3
Global coffee consumption 2012/13-2020/21 Published by Jan Conway, Feb 4, 2021
https://www.statista.com/statistics/292595/global-coffee-consumption/

America's Coffee Obsession: Fun Facts That Prove We're Hooked - Kitchen Daily
https://www.huffpost.com/entry/americas-coffee-obsession_n_987885

Chapter 5
Is Talking to yourself Healthy?
https://www.sharecare.com/health/emotional-health/article/talking-yourself-healthy

Talking to Yourself is a Sign of a Higher Intelligence (RQZ5132)
https://sites.psu.edu/ranspassionblog/2018/10/05/talking-to-yourself-is-a-sign-of-a-higher-intelligence/

Chapter 8
"Laughter is a completely social phenomenon – we are 30 times more likely to laugh if there is someone else with us" – Sophie Scott
https://www.sciencefocus.com/the-human-body/laughter-is-a-completely-social-phenomenon-we-are-30-times-more-likely-to-laugh-if-there-is-someone-else-with-us/

Do Animals Have Humor – Joseph Castro
https://www.livescience.com/60864-do-animals-have-humor.html

Laughter can keep the weight off
http://news.bbc.co.uk/2/hi/health/6274119.stm

Laughter: The Best Medicine
https://www.psychologytoday.com/us/articles/200504/laughter-the-best-medicine

You're Not Laughing Enough, and That's no Joke, Pamela Gerloff,
https://www.psychologytoday.com/ca/blog/the-possibility-paradigm/201106/youre-not-laughing-enough-and-thats-no-joke

Chapter 9
The effects of gratitude expression on neural activity
Kini P, Wong J, McInnis S, Gabana N, Brown JW. T; Neuroimage. 2016 Mar;128:1-10. doi: 10.1016/j.neuroimage.2015.12.040. Epub 2015 Dec 30. PMID: 26746580. https://pubmed.ncbi.nlm.nih.gov/26746580/